Cool FOODS
for fun fiestas

D1384631

Easy Recipes for Kids to Cook

Lisa Wagner

ABDO
Publishing Company

TO ADULT HELPERS

You're invited to assist an up-and-coming chef in a kitchen near you! And it will pay off in many ways. Your children can develop new skills, gain confidence, and make some delicious food while learning to cook. What's more, it's going to be a lot of fun!

These recipes are designed to let children cook independently as much as possible. Encourage them to do whatever they are able to do on their own. Also encourage them to try the variations supplied with each recipe and to experiment with their own ideas. Building creativity into the cooking process encourages children to think like real chefs.

Before getting started, set some ground rules about using the kitchen, cooking tools, and ingredients. Most important, adult supervision is a must whenever a child uses the stove, oven, or sharp tools. (Look for the Hot Stuff! and Super Sharp! symbols.)

So, put on your aprons and stand by. Let your young chefs take the lead. Watch and learn. Taste their creations. Praise their efforts. Enjoy the culinary adventure!

Visit us at www.abdopublishing.com

Published by ABDO Publishing Company, 4940 Viking Drive, Edina, Minnesota 55435. Copyright © 2007 by Abdo Consulting Group, Inc. International copyrights reserved in all countries. No part of this book may be reproduced in any form without written permission from the publisher. The Checkerboard Library™ is a trademark and logo of ABDO Publishing Company.

Printed in the United States.

Design and Production: Mighty Media, Inc.
Art Direction: Anders Hanson
Photo Credits: Anders Hanson, Shutterstock
Series Editor: Pam Price

The following manufacturers/names appearing in this book are trademarks: Pyrex®, Reynolds® Cut-Rite® Waxed Paper, Target® Aluminum Foil, Target® Plastic Wrap, Ortega® Refried Beans, Wesson® Corn Oil, Hellmann's® Mayonnaise, Morton® Iodized Salt

Library of Congress Cataloging-in-Publication Data

Wagner, Lisa, 1958-
  Cool foods for fun fiestas : easy recipes for kids to cook / Lisa Wagner.
    p. cm. -- (Cool cooking)
  Includes index.
  ISBN-13: 978-1-59928-722-5
  ISBN-10: 1-59928-722-6
  1. Cookery--Juvenile literature. 2. Quick and easy cookery--Juvenile literature. I. Title.

  TX652.5.W3155 2007
  641.5'622--dc22
                          2006032082

Table of Contents

What Makes Cooking So Cool

Welcome to the world of cooking! The cool thing about cooking is that you are the chef! You get to decide what to cook, how to cook, and what ingredients you want to use.

Everything you need to know to get started is in this book. You will learn the basic cooking terms and tools. All of the recipes in this book require only basic kitchen equipment. All the tools you will need are pictured on pages 8 through 9.

Most of the ingredients used in these recipes are pictured on pages 12 through 13. This will help you identify the items for your grocery list. You want to find the freshest ingredients possible when shopping. You may notice some foods marked *organic*. This means the food was grown using earth-friendly fertilizers and pest control methods.

Fiesta means "party" in Spanish. In Mexico the word *fiesta* is used for celebrations. Fiestas usually celebrate religious and national holidays. And, the party can last for several days! Colorful costumes, music, dancing, and food are part of every fiesta. But you don't have to wait for a special occasion. Turn any meal into a fiesta with foods you cook from this book!

Most of the recipes have variations, so you can be creative. A recipe can be different every time you make it. Get inspired and give a recipe your original touch. Being a cook is like being an artist in the kitchen. The most important ingredient is imagination!

GET THE PICTURE!

When a step number in a recipe has a dotted circle around it, look for the picture that goes with it. The circle around the photo will be the same color as the step number.

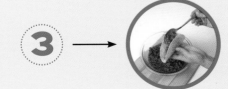

The Basics

Get going in the right direction
with a few important basics!

ASK PERMISSION

> Before you cook, get permission to use the kitchen, cooking tools, and ingredients.

> If you'd like to do everything by yourself, say so. As long as you can do it safely, do it.

> When you need help, ask. Always get help when you use the stove or oven.

BE PREPARED

> Being well organized is a chef's secret ingredient for success!

> Read through the entire recipe before you do anything else.

> Gather all your cooking tools and ingredients.

> Get the ingredients ready. The list of ingredients tells how to prepare each item.

> Put each prepared ingredient into a separate bowl.

> Read the recipe instructions carefully. Do the steps in the order they are listed.

BE SMART, BE SAFE

> If you use the stove or oven, you need an adult to stay in the kitchen with you.

> Never use the stove or oven if you are home alone!

> Always get an adult to help with the hot jobs, such as draining boiling water.

> Have an adult nearby when you are using a sharp tool such as a knife, peeler, or grater. Always use sharp tools with care.

> Always turn pot handles toward the back of the stove. This helps prevent you from accidentally knocking over pots.

> Prevent accidents by working slowly and carefully. Take your time.

> If you get hurt, let an adult know right away!

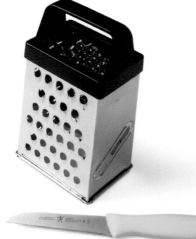

BE NEAT AND CLEAN

> Start with clean hands, clean tools, and a clean work surface.

> Tie back long hair so it stays out of the way and out of the food.

> Wear comfortable clothing and roll up your sleeves.

> Aprons and chef hats are optional!

No Germs Allowed!

After you handle raw eggs or raw meat, wash your hands with soap and water. Wash tools and work surfaces with soap and water too. Raw eggs and raw meat have **bacteria** that can't survive being cooked. But the bacteria can survive at room or body temperature. These bacteria can make you very sick if you consume them. So, keep everything clean!

MEASURING

Most ingredients are measured by the cup, tablespoon, or teaspoon.

Measuring cups and spoons come in a variety of sizes. An amount is printed or **etched** on each one to show how much it holds. To measure ½ cup, use the measuring cup marked ½ cup and fill it to the top.

Some measuring cups are large and have marks showing various amounts.

Ingredients such as meat and cheese are measured by weight in ounces or pounds. You purchase them by weight too.

KEY SYMBOLS

In this book, you will see some symbols beside the recipes. Here is what they mean.

HOT STUFF!

The recipe requires the use of a stove or oven. You need adult assistance and supervision.

SUPER SHARP!

A sharp tool such as a peeler, knife, or grater is needed. Get an adult to stand by.

EVEN COOLER!

This symbol means adventure! It could be a tip for making the recipe spicier. Sometimes it's a wild variation using an unusual ingredient. Give it a try! Get inspired and invent your own super-cool ideas.

TIP: Set a measuring cup inside a large bowl to catch spills. Hold a measuring spoon over a small bowl or cup to catch spills.

The Tool Box

A box on the bottom of the first page of each recipe lists the tools you need.
When you come across a tool you don't know, turn back to these pages.

SERRATED KNIFE

SMALL SHARP KNIFE

CUTTING BOARD

MEASURING CUPS

MEASURING SPOONS

GLASS MEASURING CUP

PREP BOWLS

MIXING BOWLS

WOODEN SPOON

SPOON

RUBBER SPATULA

TONGS

GRATER

CAN OPENER

FORK

POTATO MASHER

BAKING SHEET

SAUCEPAN

JUICER

OVEN-PROOF PLATTER

PLATE

WAXED PAPER

FRYING PAN

ALUMINUM FOIL

PLASTIC WRAP

STRAINER OR COLANDER

9 × 13 PAN

TOWELS

TIMER

POT HOLDER

PASTRY BRUSH

Cool Cooking Terms

You need to learn the basic cooking terms and the actions that go with them. Whenever you need to remind yourself, just turn back to these pages.

Most ingredients need preparation before they are cooked or assembled. Look at the list of ingredients beside the recipe. After some items, you'll see words such as *chopped*, *sliced*, or *diced*. These words tell you how to prepare the ingredients.

FIRST THINGS FIRST

Always wash fruit and vegetables well. Rinse them under cold water. Pat them dry with a towel. Then they won't slip when you cut them.

PEEL

Peel means to remove the skin. Use a peeler for carrots, potatoes, cucumbers, and apples. Hold the item to be peeled against the cutting board. Slide the peeler away from you along the surface of the food.

TIP: To peel onion or garlic, remove the papery shell. Trim each end with a sharp knife. Then peel off the outer layer with your fingers. Never put garlic or onion peels in a food disposer!

CHOP

Chop means to cut things into small pieces. The more you chop, the smaller the pieces. If a recipe says finely chopped, it means you need very small pieces.

MASH

Mash means to use the back of a fork to press down and smash the food into a paste. You can use a potato masher if you need to mash a large quantity.

CUBE OR DICE

Cube and *dice* mean to cut cube or dice shapes. Usually *dice* refers to smaller pieces, and *cube* refers to larger pieces. Often a recipe will give you a dimension, such as ¼-inch dice.

TIP: Use two steps to dice or cube. First make all your cuts going one direction. Then turn the cutting board and make the crosscuts.

SLICE

Slice means to cut food into pieces of the same thickness.

MINCE

Mince means to cut the food into the tiniest possible pieces. Garlic is often minced and sometimes onion is too.

GRATE

Grate means to shred something into small pieces using a grater. A grater has surfaces covered in holes with raised, sharp edges. You rub the food against a surface using firm pressure.

MIX

When you mix, you stir ingredients together, usually with a large spoon. *Blend* is another word for *mix*.

The Coolest Ingredients

TACO SHELLS

TORTILLA CHIPS

FLOUR TORTILLAS

CORN TORTILLAS

CHEDDAR CHEESE

MONTEREY JACK CHEESE

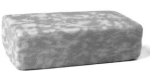

CO-JACK CHEESE

**GROUND BEEF OR
GROUND TURKEY**

TOMATO

GREEN PEPPER

JALAPEÑO PEPPERS

ICEBERG LETTUCE

CILANTRO

WHITE ONION

GARLIC

SCALLIONS

AVOCADOS

BLACK OLIVES

SALT

Get Fresh!

Dried herbs are stronger than fresh herbs. If you substitute fresh herbs for dried herbs, use at least three times as much as the recipe calls for. For example, if the recipe says 1 teaspoon dried basil, use 3 teaspoons chopped fresh basil.

CANNED REFRIED BEANS

MAYONNAISE

LEMON

LIMES

CANNED TOMATO PASTE

CANNED TOMATO PUREE

CANNED TOMATO SAUCE

SOUR CREAM

CORN OIL

OLIVE OIL

DRIED OREGANO

CHILI POWDER

GARLIC POWDER

GROUND CUMIN

SUGAR

13

Say What!

burrito *(boo-REE-toh)* – a soft flour tortilla wrapped around a filling of meat, beans, or cheese.

enchilada *(ehn-chee-LAH-dah)* – a traditional Mexican dish of tortillas dipped in chili sauce. They can be fried or baked and are often stuffed with various fillings.

fiesta *(fee-YES-tah)* – party.

guacamole *(gwok-uh-MOH-lay)* – a spread made of mashed avocado.

pico de gallo *(PEE-koh deh GUY-yo)* – literally means "rooster's beak." Perhaps the fresh salsa is called pico de gallo because the spice of the chilies makes your tongue feel as if it's been pecked by a sharp beak!

quesadilla *(kay-suh-DEE-yah)* – a fried **turnover** made of tortilla dough filled with cheese or other fillings. In the United States, quesadillas are often made with cooked tortillas instead of tortilla dough.

salsa *(SAL-suh)* – sauce.

suprema *(soo-PRAY-mah)* – supreme, the best!

tortilla *(tor-TEE-yah)* – a thin, round flat bread made of wheat or corn.

INGREDIENTS

2 very ripe medium avocados
1 small tomato, chopped
½ cup minced white onion
1 tablespoon fresh lime juice
¼ teaspoon salt

¡Olé! Guacamole

A best friend to chips and salsa!

1 Cut the avocados in half and remove the pits. Scoop the avocado from the skin and put it in a bowl.

2 Mash the avocado with a fork until it is mostly smooth.

3 Add the other ingredients and stir with the fork until blended. Serve fresh!

TOOLS:

Cutting board	Measuring spoons	Small mixing bowl
Serrated knife	Measuring cup	Fork
Small sharp knife	Prep bowls	

Cool Hot Salsas

With chips or a meal, salsa just disappears!

MAKES 2½ CUPS SALSA

INGREDIENTS

PICO DE GALLO
2 large tomatoes, chopped (about 2 cups)
½ cup chopped white onion
¼ cup chopped fresh cilantro
Juice squeezed from ½ lime
1 teaspoon olive oil
½ teaspoon salt

FRESH SALSA
2 large tomatoes, chopped (about 2 cups)
1 bunch scallions, chopped
2 garlic cloves, minced
½ green pepper, chopped
½ cup chopped fresh cilantro (or more if you like it)
1 tablespoon tomato paste
¼ cup water (use up to ½ cup if the tomatoes aren't very juicy)

TOOLS:
Cutting board
Serrated knife

Small sharp knife
Prep bowls

Small mixing bowl
Spoon

Measuring cup
Measuring spoon

1 Mix all the ingredients together in a small mixing bowl.

2 Serve right away or cover and refrigerate for up to 1 week.

TIP: A **serrated** knife is the best choice for cutting any fruit or vegetable with a firm skin and soft insides. Always use a serrated knife to cut tomatoes.

····· Variations

> Don't have any fresh tomatoes? Use canned plum tomatoes as a substitute. Just drain the canned tomatoes and chop enough to make 2 cups.

> Add chopped red peppe___ /or minced radishes.

Even Cooler!

Or in this case, even hotter! Add 1 chopped jalapeño pepper to either salsa for a spicy variation.

WARNING: Jalapeño peppers are very hot. Always wear rubber gloves when you chop jalapeño peppers. Then wash your hands, the cutting board, and the knife with soap and water right away. Be careful never to touch a cut pepper and then touch your eyes or nose. Ouch!

Tasty Tex-Mex Tacos

Absolutely awesome tacos!

MAKES 12 TACOS

INGREDIENTS

12 taco shells

TACO FILLING

1 pound ground beef or turkey

1 cup chopped white onion

1 clove garlic, minced

1 8-ounce can tomato sauce

⅓ cup water

¾ teaspoon salt

1 tablespoon chili powder

½ teaspoon dried oregano

½ teaspoon ground cumin

GARNISHES

½ head iceberg lettuce, cut in ¼-inch strips

1 large tomato, diced

1 cup fresh salsa or pico de gallo (page 16)

1½ cups grated Cheddar or co-jack cheese

TOOLS:
Cutting board
Serrated knife
Small sharp knife
Measuring spoons

Measuring cups
Prep bowls
Can opener
Frying pan

Wooden spoon
Grater
Pot holder
Baking sheet

Tongs

TO MAKE THE FILLING

1 Put the ground meat, onion, and garlic in a frying pan. Cook over medium-high heat. As the meat browns, break it up with a wooden spoon so it cooks evenly. Cook until all the pink color is gone from the meat.

2 Have an adult help you drain the grease from the pan.

3 Stir in the tomato sauce, water, salt, and spices. Cook over medium heat for 5 to 10 minutes, stirring occasionally.

TO WARM THE TACO SHELLS

1 Put the taco shells on a baking sheet.

2 Warm the shells in a preheated, 350-degree oven for 3 minutes.

3 Remove the shells from the oven and use tongs to gently put them on a platter.

TO SERVE

1 Put 2 tablespoons of the meat filling in each shell. Take the serving platter to the table.

2 Put bowls of lettuce, tomato, salsa, and grated cheese on the table. Let everyone make their own tacos using the **garnishes** they like best.

Fiesta Nachos

Turn snack time into fiesta time!

MAKES ENOUGH FOR 4 PEOPLE

INGREDIENTS

8 5-inch corn tortillas

2 tablespoons corn oil or canola oil

3 cups grated Cheddar or co-jack cheese

TOOLS: Measuring cups · Measuring spoons · Cutting board · Small sharp knife · Pastry brush · Grater · Baking sheet · Oven-proof platter · Pot holder · Tongs

1 Preheat oven to 425 degrees.

2 Brush both sides of each tortilla lightly with oil.

3 Cut each tortilla into 6 triangles.

4 Put the tortilla triangles on a baking sheet and bake them in the oven for 5 minutes. Remove the baking sheet from the oven and turn the triangles over with tongs. Put the baking sheet back in the oven and bake for 5 more minutes. Remove the tortilla chips from the oven and let them cool.

5 Arrange the tortilla chips on an oven-proof platter. Cover them with the grated cheese.

6 Put the platter in the oven and bake until the cheese is bubbly, about 5 minutes.

7 Let the nachos cool slightly before serving them. Be careful, the platter will still be hot!

8 Serve with fresh salsa or pico de gallo (page 16) and guacamole (page 15).

Variations

> For speedy nachos, and no hot platter, use a microwave oven to melt the cheese. Start with 1 minute on high power. Then turn the platter to help the cheese melt evenly. Continue to cook in 30-second **increments** until the cheese is melted.

> Create your own nachos with different toppings. Try chopped scallions, chopped black olives, diced tomatoes, diced cooked chicken, refried beans, or taco meat.

Beautiful Burritos

*Wrap up a delicious
meal or snack!*

MAKES 8 BURRITOS

INGREDIENTS

8 6-inch round flour tortillas

BEAN BURRITO FILLING

1 16-ounce can refried beans

½ cup chopped white onion

1 tablespoon sour cream

½ teaspoon garlic powder

1 teaspoon chili powder

1 teaspoon ground cumin

½ teaspoon salt

2 cups grated cheese (Cheddar,
Monterey Jack or co-jack)

GARNISHES

Fresh salsa or pico de gallo
(page 16)

Sour cream

Black olives

Chopped scallions

TOOLS: Cutting board   Can opener   Spoon   Tongs   9 × 13 pan
Small sharp knife   Prep bowls   Grater   Plate
Measuring spoons   Mixing bowl   Pot holder   Towel
Measuring cups   Fork   Frying pan   Aluminum foil

1 Preheat oven to 325 degrees.

2 Set a frying pan on the stove over medium-high heat. Soften the tortillas by warming them for 30 seconds on each side. Turn the tortillas with tongs. After warming them, put the tortillas on a plate and cover them with a towel until you are ready to fill them.

3 Put the beans in a mixing bowl and mash them with a fork until they're smooth. Add the rest of the ingredients except the grated cheese and mix until they're well blended.

4 Put ¼ cup of the bean mixture in the center of a tortilla. Sprinkle ¼ cup of grated cheese on top of the beans.

5 Fold in one side of the tortilla by 1 inch.

6 Fold the side of the tortilla closest to you over the middle. Be sure the folded edge stays inside.

7 Roll the tortilla over one more time, and you have a burrito!

8 Put the burritos in a 9 × 13 pan. Cover them with aluminum foil and bake for 20 minutes.

Even Cooler!

Add 1 teaspoon of pepper sauce for a spicy filling. Want it even hotter? Add 1 chopped jalapeño pepper (see page 17).

Layered Fiesta Dip

Seven layers of flavor!

MAKES ABOUT 10 CUPS

INGREDIENTS

2 cups bean burrito filling (page 22)
2 cups guacamole (page 15)
1 cup sour cream
2 teaspoons chili powder
1 bunch scallions, chopped
1 cup sliced black olives
2 cups fresh salsa (page 16)
1½ cups grated Cheddar cheese
1 bag tortilla chips

TOOLS: Cutting board, Small sharp knife | Can opener, Measuring cups | Measuring spoons, Prep bowls | Grater, Rubber spatula | 9 × 13 pan, Plastic wrap

1. Spread the bean dip in an even layer on the bottom of the baking pan. Smooth the surface with a spatula.

2. To create the layers, spread or sprinkle the other ingredients evenly over the beans one ingredient at a time. Add the ingredients in the order they are listed.

3. Cover the pan with plastic wrap and refrigerate it for an hour before serving.

4. Serve with tortilla chips on the side for dipping.

Variations

> Try Monterey Jack or co-jack cheese instead of Cheddar.

> Use 1 large chopped tomato (about 1 cup) instead of the salsa. Serve the salsa on the side instead.

> In a hurry? Use prepared bean dip, guacamole, and salsa from the grocery store.

Baked Quesadillas

Quick, cheesy and plenty easy!

MAKES 8 QUESADILLAS

INGREDIENTS

8 8-inch flour tortillas

4 cups grated Cheddar or Monterey Jack cheese

Corn oil

GARNISHES

Fresh salsa or pico de gallo (page 16)

Guacamole (page 15)

Sour cream

TOOLS: Grater
Large mixing bowl
Measuring cups

Waxed paper
Baking sheet
Pot holder

Tongs
Aluminum foil

1. Preheat the oven to 425 degrees.

2. Use waxed paper to spread a thin layer of corn oil on the baking sheet.

3. Put two tortillas on the baking sheet. Sprinkle ½ cup of cheese on each tortilla. Don't spread it all the way to the edge. Leave about ½ inch of tortilla showing all the way around.

4. Bake the quesadillas for about 5 minutes, or until the cheese is melted.

5. Use tongs to fold the tortillas in half. Then put them on a serving platter and cover them with foil to keep them warm.

6. Make the other batches following steps 3 through 5.

7. Serve with **garnishes** on the side.

Variations

> Add chopped scallions, chopped canned green chilies, cooked diced chicken, or cooked taco meat.

Even Cooler!

For giant quesadillas, use 12-inch tortillas. Use 1 cup of cheese for each quesadilla and bake them one at a time on a round pizza pan. Cut them into wedges and serve.

Enchiladas Supremas

Bet these are the best enchiladas you ever tasted!

MAKES 8 ENCHILADAS

INGREDIENTS

8 corn tortillas
5 cups grated Cheddar cheese

ENCHILADA SAUCE

1 tablespoon corn oil
1 cup minced white onion
1 clove garlic, minced
1 28-ounce can tomato puree
1 cup water
2 tablespoons chili powder
½ teaspoon ground cumin
½ teaspoon dried oregano
½ teaspoon salt

GARNISHES

1 bunch scallions, chopped
Sour cream

TOOLS:	Cutting board	Measuring cups	Can opener	Wooden spoon	9 × 13 pan
	Small sharp knife	Prep bowls	Saucepan with cover	Tongs	Pot holder
	Measuring spoons	Grater	Frying pan	Towel	

TO MAKE THE SAUCE

1 Heat the oil in a medium saucepan and add the onion and garlic. Stir occasionally with a wooden spoon. Cook over medium heat for about 5 minutes.

2 Add the tomato **puree**, water, and spices. Mix until everything is well blended.

3 Turn the heat to medium low. Cover the saucepan and cook for 20 minutes. Stir often with a wooden spoon.

4 Remove the pan from the heat.

TO BUILD THE ENCHILADAS

1 Preheat oven to 350 degrees.

2 Set a frying pan on the stove over medium-high heat. Soften the tortillas by warming them for 30 seconds on each side. Turn the tortilla with tongs. After warming them, put the tortillas on a plate and cover them with a towel until you are ready to fill them.

3 Using the tongs, dip one tortilla into the sauce mixture. Make sure it is well coated.

4 Put the tortilla on the cutting board and put ½ cup of cheese in the middle.

5 Roll the tortilla to close it and place it seam down in the baking pan.

6 Repeat steps 2 through 4 with the rest of the tortillas.

7 Pour the remaining sauce evenly over all the enchiladas in the baking pan.

8 Bake uncovered in the oven for 15 minutes. Remove the pan from the oven and sprinkle the remaining cup of cheese over the top.

9 Return the pan to the oven for 5 more minutes.

10 Sprinkle chopped scallions over the top and serve with sour cream on the side.

Variations

> For chicken and cheese enchiladas, fill each tortilla with ¼ cup diced cooked chicken and ¼ cup cheese.

> In a hurry? Use canned enchilada sauce from the grocery store.

Glossary

bacteria – tiny, one-celled organisms that can only be seen through a microscope.

etch – to cut a pattern into a surface with acid or a laser.

garnish – something used to decorate food or drink.

increment – a small increase in amount or value.

puree – food that is finely ground to make a paste or a thick liquid.

serrated – having a jagged edge.

turnover – a filled pastry made by folding the crust in half with the filling inside.

Web Sites

To learn more about cool cooking, visit ABDO Publishing Company on the World Wide Web at **www.abdopublishing.com**. Web sites about cool cooking are featured on our Book Links page. These links are routinely monitored and updated to provide the most current information available.

Index